50**ESSENTIAL**WARM-UPS

FORDRUMS

Powerful Drum Exercises to Improve Control, Speed and Endurance

KEV**O'SHEA**

FUNDAMENTAL**CHANGES**

50 Essential Warm-ups for Drums

Powerful Drum Exercises to Improve Control, Speed and Endurance

ISBN: 978-1-911267-58-4

Published by **www.fundamental-changes.com**

www.fundamental-changes.com

Twitter: @guitar_joseph

Over 10,000 fans on Facebook: **FundamentalChangesInGuitar**

Instagram: **FundamentalChanges**

For over 350 Free Guitar Lessons with Videos Check Out

www.fundamental-changes.com

Cover Image Copyright: Shutterstock – Prathan Nakdontree

Contents

Introduction 5

How to Use the BPM Suggestions 6

Stretching 7

    Stretch One: Fingers and Wrists 7

    Stretch Two: Rotation 8

Essential Techniques for Warmups 9

    Pull-out Accents 9

    Finger Stroke 10

    Flams 11

    Snaps 11

Get the Audio 12

50 Essential Warm-ups for Drums 13

1: The Snap 14

2: The Pendulum 15

3: Four Stroke Ruff 16

4: Inverted Double Eights 17

5: Triple Strokes 18

6: Flam Accent Variation 19

7: The Snapadiddle 20

8: The Quintessential 21

9: Triples over 4 22

10: One-sided Hertas 23

11: Pull-out accents in 12/8 24

12: On-off Flam Accent 25

13: The Mixer 26

14: Herta Fly 27

15: Herbie 28

16: Snapadiddle Inversion #1 29

17: The Tightrope 30

18: The Cuckoo 31

19: Double snaps 32

20: The Riffle 33

21: Hyper-Bolero 34

22: 12/8 Pull-out Accents 35

23: Snapadiddle Inversion #2 36

24: The Flutter-By 37

25: The Hustle 38

26: Foreign Flam Accent 39

27: Snap Accent Run 40

28: Singles On The Rebound 41

29: Single Stroke Workout #1 42

30: Marching With The Ruffs 43

31: Herbie Returns 44

32: The Juggler 45

33: Quincey 46

34: 12/8 Off-beat Pull-outs 47

35: Snapadiddle Inversion #3 48

36: Single Stroke Workout #2 49

37: Consecutive Flam 4's 50

38: Inverted Doubles Run 51

39: Herta Dublin 52

40: Pulling Teeth 53

41: Flamming Moe 54

42: 12/8 Switcheroo 55

43: Snappled 56

44: Parsnaps 57

45: The Blender 58

46: Trippin' Sevens 59

47: Inverted Seven 60

48: Inverted Swiss Variation 61

49: Flam Central 62

50: Single Stroke Workout #3 63

Conclusion 64

    Further Reading 64

About the Author 65

Other Books from Fundamental Changes 66

Introduction

50 Essential Warmups For Drums contains a collection of the best sticking exercises for use as warm-ups and technique-builders before drumming. They are designed to be learnt on the practice pad before transferring them to the drum kit.

It is intended that you read through the whole book, attempting each example before moving to the next. After some time, you can use it to selectively choose a warm-up before a gig or a session depending on what you feel would be most beneficial for you.

I recommend that you spend at least 3-5 minutes on each pattern at both slow and fast tempos. Always play relaxed and focus on clarity and precision. Stay relaxed because tension is harmful to your joints and tendons.

Be aware of your stick size in relation to your arm length. The right sized stick should feel like a comfortable extension of the forearm, particularly in weight. A stick which is too big or too small can put unnecessary demands on your joints when you strike the drums hard.

To really benefit from these exercises, it is important to learn each one to the level where you do not have to read the notation, count, or think about the sticking. You can then enter an almost a trance-like state. Let the blood flow, breathe deeply, and your hands will loosen up.

Each warm-up is notated over two bars. Some warm-ups are two-bar phrases, others are one-bar phrases with 'reversed' sticking notated in the second bar. With the latter, simply pause and switch hands after mastering the initial sticking.

One-bar phrases are easily identified by a double bar line. Two-bar phrases are sometimes referred to as 'symmetrical', as the sticking naturally switches the leading hand from the first bar to the second, then back again on the repeat.

Some exercises have accents notated, others do not. Quite often, accents can be played at your discretion. If you choose to add or remove accents to make the examples easier to play that is perfectly acceptable, so long as you return to master both the original notation as well as your variation. This will give you the greatest benefit in the long-run.

Listen along to the audio examples supplied with this book. If you haven't yet downloaded the accompanying audio you can do so by following the instructions in the 'Get the Audio' section below. Understanding how a written exercise sounds and *feels* will greatly increase your benefit from this book.

How to Use the BPM Suggestions

Throughout this book you will have noticed that each exercise has a suggested Beats Per Minute (BPM) range to play within. This is an indicator of what metronome settings you should use.

In 4/4 exercises, the BPM refers to the quarter note pulse. In other time signatures like 12/8, 7/8 or 5/8, the BPM may represent groups of two or three 1/8th notes. Use the accompanying audio as a guide.

It makes sense when getting to grips with a warm-up to take it slowly and strive for accuracy. At lower tempos, it's often easier to use your wrists and arm to produce the strokes. Conversely, at higher tempos, the smaller muscle groups such as the fingers will allow greater speed and more nuanced control.

Make a note of the tempo you are comfortable with on each example. For an added challenge, note down your own personal best speeds and work towards beating them each time you revisit the exercise.

You'll often find that if you can play a warm-up cleanly at a high tempo for a minute or so, it's usually easy enough to raise the tempo by five or ten BPM. You might not have the stamina or technique to maintain this new tempo for long, but that will develop with time and practice.

Stretching

The following stretches are a recommended before you begin to play. The first stretch focuses on the fingers and wrists.

Stretch One: Fingers and Wrists

- While holding either end of both sticks with your palms facing upwards, lift your fists up and continue this motion back towards your chest.

- Keep all fingers around the stick in a loose and relaxed manner. If you feel any pain at all stop immediately.

- Continue this rotational movement until you end up with a clear view of the back of your hands which are both still holding the stick. See figure 1 for a visual demonstration.

Figure 1

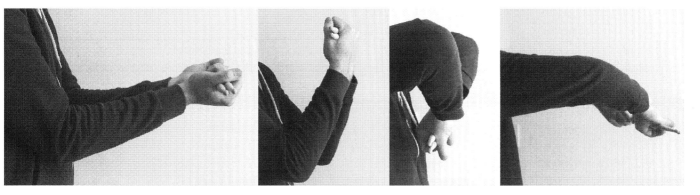

- Be careful not to strain here. If it feels uncomfortable you may need to start again by gripping the sticks with your hands further apart. Simply breathe in and out several times and let the hands adjust. After around 10-15 seconds release the little (pinky) finger.

- Remain loose and relaxed and let the stick do the work. The important thing about these stretches is not to be forceful; rather it is to hold the correct position long enough for the body to adjust.

- Release the ring finger.

- Hold for around 10-15 seconds and then release the middle finger.

- Figure 2 shows the different finger stretches in more detail.

Figure 2.

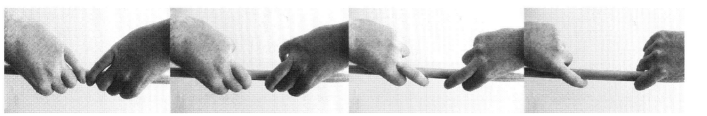

When you are done, shake the hands loose and move on to the following exercise.

Stretch Two: Rotation

- Hold both sticks in one hand by the tip as shown in figure 3.

- Keep your arm extended out from the body at all times.

- The motion required here is a rotation of approximately 180 degrees before returning to the starting position.

- Turn from the elbow to create an almost windscreen (windshield) wiper effect.

- Rotate about 10 times with each arm and then repeat.

- Let the weight of the sticks stretch your arm lightly with each turn.

Figure 3.

Essential Techniques for Warmups

Pull-out Accents

Pull-out accents require a technique that consists of two parts. The first part is a regular 'tap' stroke and the second part is an accent which comes from a wrist & forearm down-stroke. The tricky part is getting from the initial tap to the 'up' position so that you can play the full down-stroke.

- First, hold the stick about 2-3 inches over the surface of the head or pad.

- Next lift the forearm from the elbow and let your wrist go slack to allow the stick to move downwards to tap the head.

- The movement of the forearm upwards should 'whip' the wrist into the 'up' position after playing the initial stroke.

Figure 4 shows the positions from pre-tap stroke to tap stroke to the up position. In the up position, you are ready to play the accent.

Figure 4.

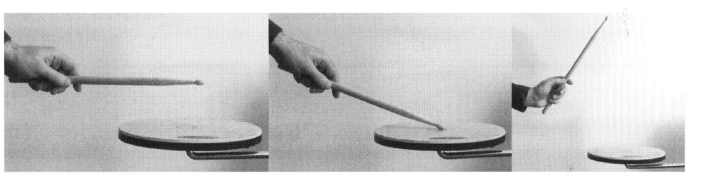

Pull-out accents are difficult to master but you will find that they work an entirely different muscle group and provide new challenges. The long-term benefits are more power and speed around the drums.

Finger Stroke

As it implies, the finger stroke comes directly from the fingers as opposed to the wrist alone. Try to keep all fingers in contact with the stick when performing this stroke. The fulcrum should be between thumb and forefinger, with all four fingers controlling the movement of the stick.

Here is an example of a finger stroke in a 'French-style' grip.

Figure 5.

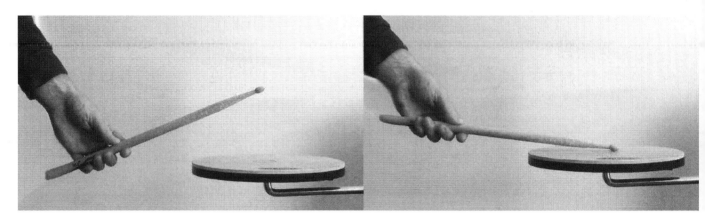

Notice the placement of the thumb is on top of the stick. This grip combined with fingers can produce a double with a down/up movement from wrist and forearm.

When playing simple wrist taps in French grip you can use a wrist turning motion (similar to turning a door knob) for extra power and speed.

The following image shows the use of fingers in a 'German-style' grip which is predominantly 'palm down'. Notice the difference between the finger stroke in French and German grips.

The thumb ends up at the side of the stick in German but on top of the stick in French.

Figure 6.

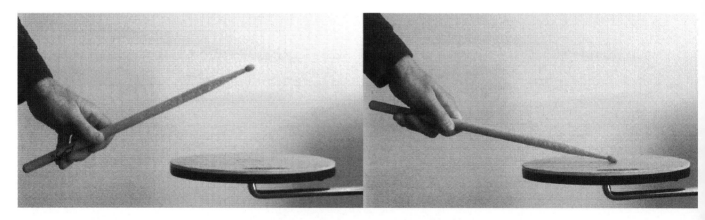

I find I use French or German grips in different situations on the kit. It usually comes down to what feels most comfortable reach-wise.

Flams

Flams are made up of a normal stroke preceded by a grace note (a light tap). This grace note embellishes the following full stroke. Here is how a right-handed flam is notated on the staff:

Figure 7.

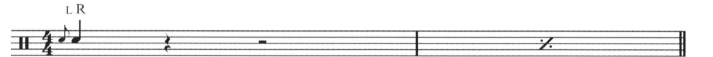

Snaps

Snaps are when we fill in a regular double stroke with an extra tap from the other hand. Snaps are usually played without accents but accents can be added to either the first or last note of the three.

Figure 8.

Get the Audio

The audio files for this book are available to download for free from **www.fundamental-changes.com** and the link is in the top right corner. Simply select this book title from the drop-down menu and follow the instructions to get the audio.

We recommend that you download the files directly to your computer, not to your tablet, and extract them there before adding them to your media library. You can then put them on your tablet, iPod or burn them to CD. On the download page, there is a help PDF and we also provide technical support via the contact form.

Twitter: **@guitar_joseph**

FB: **FundamentalChangesInGuitar**

Instagram: **FundamentalChanges**

50 Essential Warm-ups for Drums

1: The Snap

(One-bar phrase)

A fundamental exercise that will form the basis of many warm-ups. I call this 'The Snap' and it is treated like a double stroke with an extra note in between.

At lower speeds you can play this exercise with full down-strokes. At higher speeds it is more beneficial to use the wrist followed by fingers for each double stroke.

On the drum set, you can move the three-note pattern between different voices to increase accuracy.

Moving from snare to hi-hat, and from the floor tom to front tom works well here.

Suggested BPM range: 140-280

2: The Pendulum

(Two-bar phrase)

A symmetrical exercise that focuses on groups of dotted 1/8th note triplets. You can play this with, or without accents.

When playing without accents, switch between the above phrase and two bars of 'hand-to-hand 1/16ths' while trying to keep the dynamics as even as possible.

On the kit, you can move the accented hand around to create interesting patterns. There is potential for some tricky cross sticking as you move the left-hand accent around the drums.

Try substituting the accent for bass drum and crash cymbal together.

Suggested BPM range: 80-160

3: Four Stroke Ruff

(One-bar phrase)

R L R L R   L R L R   L R L R   L R L   L   R L R L   R L R L   R L R L   R L R

The 'four stroke ruff' or 'single stroke four'.

Another fundamental bit-part of future exercises. The ruff can be played with increasing tempo from first stroke to the last. In the audio example, we treat the ruff as four equal strokes.

At slow tempos, be clear and precise. At faster tempos, treat the exercise as a double stroke in both hands. These double strokes are staggered to create four separate notes.

When applied to the drums, you can create a wide range of musical ideas. One simple application is to try moving the last note of the ruff to a tom or cymbal. A different kind of motion is required here as you will need to use the upper arm in conjunction with the wrist and fingers to reach the tom or cymbal.

Suggested BPM range: 90-180

4: Inverted Double Eights

(One-bar phrase)

Introducing inverted double strokes.

The key here is to try to make the inverted doubles as even as possible. Play this exercise with and without accents. Doubles can also be played with a wrist/ finger combination. This technique can be more effective on different surfaces like toms and cymbals.

It's quite easy to apply this pattern to a kick, snare and hi-hat drum beat. Using the right-handed sticking, play each right-hand on the hi-hat and each left-hand on the snare. You can add a bass drum to beat 1 to create an interesting halftime pattern.

Suggested BPM range: 90-180

5: Triple Strokes

(One-bar phrase)

Three even strokes on each hand.

It's important to practise starting on both hands here as it requires a mental shift in emphasis.

The triple stroke will be applied to future exercises such as singles and flams.

Take this pattern around the drums, from snare to toms and cymbals.

You might need to adjust your technique to get three full strokes on different surfaces. Open the snare and move your hands around the drums only to create a tribal 12/8 pattern.

Suggested BPM range: 90-180

6: Flam Accent Variation

(Two-bar phrase)

A variation on the flam accent that turns the phrase into a symmetrical exercise.

The last three notes of the bar are worth paying attention to. It is these three notes that allow the sticking to easily switch hands into the next bar.

Incorporating toms is a nice way to apply this warm-up to the drum kit. Try playing each grace note as a tom while keeping your snare for the regular 1/8th note strokes. For example, the first left-handed grace note could be shifted to the floor tom on a regular right-handed drum set up.

Use this approach to add colour to the pattern. Before you know it, there is a world of flam fills waiting to be discovered.

Suggested BPM range: 80-160

7: The Snapadiddle

(One-bar phrase)

The 'Snapadiddle'.

If you are already familiar with the paradiddle then this concept should come easily. An extra note is to be played between the double stroke of a regular paradiddle.

I like to play this warm-up on the hi-hat in a regular 4/4 beat.

With the bass drum on beat 1, you can move the left-hand on beat 3 to the snare to create a halftime back beat feel.

For an added challenge move your right hand to the ride cymbal while keeping your left on hi-hat and snare.

This pattern can also be used with reverse sticking. In that case, it is the right-hand that plays the snare drum back beat.

Suggested BPM range: 110-220

8: The Quintessential

(Two-bar phrase)

This warm-up is in 5/8. You don't necessarily need to count this exercise but it is easier to notate it this way. A six-stroke roll followed by a paradiddle which reverses the exercise to the other hand.

If you were you to count this exercise in 1/8th notes you would find the accents land on beats 1 and 4.

When taking this exercise to the drum set you can play it between ride cymbal and hi-hat. Play the right-hand accents together with the bell of the ride and the bass drum for more definition.

Next, play the left-hand accents on the snare to create an interesting 5/8 or 5/4 groove.

Suggested BPM range: 1/4 notes @ 100-190

9: Triples over 4

(Two-bar phrase)

R R R L L L R R R L L L R R L R   L L L R R R L L L R R R L L R L

Triple strokes and doubles combined over a two-bar phrase.

Sticking is reversed in the second bar. Play at low tempos with an emphasis on even sounding notes before you increase speed.

This is a great exercise to play around the kit while moving the sticking between different drums. Aim for three even-sounding notes for each triple stroke.

Suggested BPM range: 70-130

10: One-sided Hertas

(One-bar phrase)

R L R R L R L L R L R R R L R L L   L R L L R L R R R L R L L R L R R

Triple strokes combining with snaps.

This exercise is in 12/ 8. There is no need to play accents here, just focus on accurate placement of the additional note in each three-note grouping.

For an added challenge, take this warm-up to the drum set and play between the toms and snare. Try placing the first note of each grouping onto a tom and play the following notes on the snare.

Now reverse the voicing so that you play the first note on the snare and the following notes on any tom of your choice.

This is a rigorous workout for arms and wrists. Focus on hitting the direct centre of each drum to improve accuracy.

Suggested BPM range: 70-140

11: Pull-out Accents in 12/8

(One-bar phrase)

Introduction to 'pull-out' accents.

Pull-out accents are great for increasing lower arm control and power. See the introduction section for a deeper explanation. I recommend keeping to a low tempo with this exercise for as long as possible. Perfecting the transition from tap to down-stroke accent is the key, and only comes with repetition.

One helpful way to get comfortable with pull-out accents is to use another drum to play the notated accents. By shifting your hand from snare to tom to play the accent, you will automatically have to use the upper arm. It is the movement of the upper arm that will be the key to producing a strong second accented note.

For convenience, play each right-handed accent on the floor tom and each left-hand on the hi-hat. This suggested sticking is when dealing with an orthodox right-handed kit setup.

Suggested BPM range: 40-80

12: On-off Flam Accent

(One-bar phrase)

Consecutive flams.

Here we delay a regular flam accent by two 1/8th notes to create a more difficult exercise. This pattern is not symmetrical so be sure to reverse the sticking.

Apart from moving the grace notes to other drums, like toms, you can also reverse this concept and shift the note that *follows* each grace note. In this case, the first right-hand can play a crash cymbal with bass drum underneath. The left-hand grace note will stay in the position over the snare.

Do this for all flams in the pattern.

The consecutive flams in the final and first beats in the bar will be the trickiest to master, so take your time and keep the tempo down until you are comfortable with the sticking.

Suggested BPM range: 60-150

13: The Mixer

(One-bar phrase)

Based on 'the ruff' or the 'single stroke four', this is a hand-to-hand exercise in 12/8.

Essentially it is a five-note phrase that is played from hand to hand.

Adding accents to each 1/8th note is optional so be aware of what you find more difficult to play and work on it.

The Mixer works well as a Buddy Rich-style big band lick. Substitute the first note of each five-note grouping to crash and bass drum. In 12/8 this will mean playing beats 1, 4, 7 and 10.

When you have mastered this concept, you can move onto other variations of The Mixer.

Try playing the last note of each four-note ruff with crash cymbal and bass drum. In this case, we are accenting beats 3, 6, 9 and 12.

Suggested BPM range: 40-120

14: Herta Fly

(Two-bar phrase)

A symmetrical phrase demonstrated with rim-shots on the audio example.

This is a good one to play out for 3-5 minutes in a relaxed state.

You can use this pattern to play triplets around the kit. Essentially this warm-up is an easy way of working on 'Hertas' while leading with either left or right-hand.

The three 1/8th notes at the end of each bar allow the sticking to easily reverse.

Suggested BPM range: 70-160

15: Herbie

(One-bar phrase)

Single strokes in 12/8 that resolve to switch hands every beat.

This exercise is a progression from the earlier triple-stroke patterns in warm-ups #5 and #10. Treat it in the same way and aim for three even strokes in each leading hand. The extra strokes can be added in with the opposite hand later.

When taking this exercise to a five-piece drum set you can split the pattern evenly into 4 beats. Beats 1-3 will have five notes. Beat 4 will have three notes.

A handy application of this method is to play beat 1 on the floor tom. Next move up to your front tom for beat 2. Beat 3 can be played on the middle tom which is now easily accessed with your right-hand.

Finally, play the three strokes of beat 4 on the snare.

By using this method and repeating it with reverse sticking you can find new, interesting ways to voice the warm-up.

Suggested BPM range: 70-140

16: Snapadiddle Inversion #1

(One-bar phrase)

Inverting the Snapadiddle.

Start with a regular inverted paradiddle to get a steady flow (a double-stroke followed by two singles played straight as 1/8th notes). Next add the extra note between each double stroke.

I like to play this warmup between tom and snare as it creates some tricky movements to explore.

Play the first three-note grouping on the snare then move to the tom to play the next two 1/8th notes. Continue with this movement as the sticking reverses.

When you have mastered this iteration, try starting the pattern on the tom instead. This time you will move from tom to snare and back. Be sure to aim for the centre of each drum to avoid sloppiness.

Always favour accuracy over speed because the speed will come naturally in time.

Suggested BPM range: 110-220

17: The Tightrope

(Two-bar phrase)

Transitioning triple strokes with double strokes.

A great warm-up for loosening the fingers.

Consistent stick height will lead to consistent volume. Try to keep the notes as even as possible and the tempo steady.

You can use this exercise on the drum set by orchestrating it between ride cymbal and snare for your right and left-hands respectively.

For an added challenge, add a bass drum on each ride cymbal.

Suggested BPM range: 70-180

18: The Cuckoo

(Two-bar phrase)

A mix of some 'Swiss Army Triplets' and a 'Flam Tap' to create a warm-up in 11/8.

Three groups of three and one group of two make the eleven.

Aim for full sounding flams - not 'flat' or in unison.

This is another great flam exercise to take to the kit and add extra voices like toms and cymbals.

Suggested BPM range: 1/4 note = 55-110

19: Double snaps

(One-bar phrase)

R L L R R L L R L R L L R R L L R L   L R R L L R R L R L R R L L R R L R

Adding snaps to inverted doubles.

Start slow; feel the rhythm before you try to increase the tempo. If you don't have a solid grasp of the inverted pulse things can get messy.

When happy with your consistent sticking, stop and switch hands.

When applying this pattern to the drums use beat 1 and beat 3 to change up the voicing. Adding accents like rim-shots works well here. Also, you can use this warm-up to create a halftime pattern. Start on the hi-hat and add a bass drum to beat 1.

Next, aim to move your right-hand down to the snare on just beat 3. Play at a slow tempo first to establish the rhythm correctly.

When you have mastered this halftime groove, switch it up by adding more bass drum hits throughout the bar. Beat 2 and 4 would be an obvious next choice.

Suggested BPM range: 70-140

20: The Riffle

(One-bar phrase)

R l l r r l l r r L R l l r r L   L r r l l r r l l R L r r l l R

Combining accents with inverted doubles.

This is not a symmetrical exercise.

This warm-up could be seen as an inverted ten-stroke roll plus an inverted 6 stroke roll that makes one bar of 1/16ths in 4/4.

You can use this warm-up to create blazing snare and tom fills. For example, when playing this pattern with a right-hand lead we will play all right-hand accents on the floor tom. Each left-hand can be played on another tom to start with.

This exercise also works well when you substitute the accents for crash and bass drum combinations.

Suggested BPM range: 90-190

21: Hyper-Bolero

(Two-bar phrase)

A more musical example of the four-stroke ruff played as a triplet within a triplet. Stop, switch hands and resume.

A great way to incorporate this exercise into your kit playing is to experiment with the 1/8th note placement. Keep each triplet on the snare drum and move the accents to toms and cymbals.

Returning your hands to the correct position after playing the accents can be a challenge at higher speeds.

Suggested BPM range: 60-130

FOLLOW US ON
INSTAGRAM
@KindergartenEducation

THIS NOTEBOOK BELONGS TO:

MORE BOOKS BY SMART KIDS NOTEBOOKS

TRACE THE LINE
TO CONNECT BOTH SIDES

TRACE THE LINE
TO CONNECT BOTH SIDES

TRACE THE SHAPES

22: 12/8 Pull-out Accents

(One-bar phrase)

Adding accents and snaps to inverted doubles in 12/8.

The nice thing about doubles played this way is that they automatically alternate hands every two beats.

Pay attention to stick height to create a strong accent. There needs to be a whipping motion upwards from the tap (first stroke of the double) to get the height required for the accent (the second stroke).

This whipping motion comes from the arm and assists the natural rebound of the first hit.

For added difficulty on the kit, play the 1/16th note section between the snare and the first tom. This will mean playing each note on the snare *apart* from the accent, which should be played on the tom of your choice.

Start at a slow tempo to ensure proper accuracy with your stick placement. It's important to strike the centre of each drum.

Never sacrifice accuracy for speed early on when learning this technique.

Suggested BPM range: 40-90

23: Snapadiddle Inversion #2

(One-bar phrase)

Taking the Snapadiddle through another inversion.

A great exercise to use between hi-hat and snare especially with the back beat on 3.

This time the 'snap' lands on the offbeat of beats 1 and 3. You can count this warm-up "1-and-a-2-and-3-and-a-4-and". Repeat on the opposite hand.

You might want to experiment by starting this application on your weaker hand. In a standard drum setup, this means you can play beat 3 with your leading hand and avoid any awkward crossing of hands.

It's good practice to get comfortable with leading with the opposite hand. Practise this exercise with bass drum hits on a mixture of beats 1, 2 and 4.

This pattern could also be played at double the tempo with a combination of 1/16th notes and 1/32nd notes.

Suggested BPM range: 110-220

24: The Flutter-By

(One-bar phrase)

Inverted doubles and a flam in 5/8.

If you were to count this exercise as 1/8th notes then the flam would land on beat 5. Adding the accent to beat 1 is optional. For added difficulty try playing this symmetrically as a two-bar phrase.

To apply this pattern to the drum set it's helpful to get comfortable with hearing it as if written over one beat. When you have mastered the sticking, you can then start to place a bass drum pulse on the first beat of each 5/8 bar.

By increasing the speed, it becomes easier to hear this warm-up as a one-beat phrase that contains a flurry of notes.

This pattern works well in a typical 12/8 blues beat at slow to moderate tempos. In this case, you should play the pattern over each three-note pulse.

Suggested BPM range: 80-120

25: The Hustle

(Two-bar phrase)

Quadruple strokes with snaps.

Here we have groups of four, three and two in each hand to create a symmetrical exercise. This is a great warm-up for the fingers.

When you are comfortable playing this warm-up on the pad or snare drum, it's a good idea to see how you fare on other surfaces. Playing between floor tom and front tom will really test your technique and build stamina in the wrists and fingers.

On lower tuned toms, you will need to harness the power of the fingers to continue the bounce at higher speeds. On high tuned toms, there will be more bounce to play with.

Suggested BPM range: 60-110

26: Foreign Flam Accent

(One-bar phrase)

5/8 flam exercise.

The consecutive flams in this exercise are followed by two flam accents.

Practise a run of alternating flams before you attempt this warm-up. This will make reversing the sticking a bit easier.

This warm-up can be played between hi-hat and snare for a busy off-time sounding drum fill.

The key is to start by learning the pattern solely on the snare drum.

Next, play each flam between hi-hat and snare. To do this you must keep the grace note on the snare while moving the full stroke to the hi-hat. Do this for each flam. You can work this pattern into a regular 4/4 beat to give a disjointed feel.

In order to keep the 4/4 timing, play six additional 1/16th notes at the end of the phrase.

Suggested BPM range: 1/4 note @ 50-120

27: Snap Accent Run

(Two-bar phrase)

Inverted doubles with accented snaps.

This is a great warm-up to try out on the hi-hats. Aim to play the accents on the edge of the hi-hat and every other stroke on the hi-hat surface. This requires a bit more co-ordination than on a single drum or practise pad.

Suggested BPM range: 60-130

28: Singles On The Rebound

(One-bar phrase)

Double strokes with hand-to-hand accents.

Aim for a low stick height with each double and a high stick height for each accent.

It's important to strive for clean and even double strokes. If your doubles are weak and unsteady they won't cut through your playing on the drum set.

Pay close attention to the second stroke of each double and work on any weaknesses there.

Practise substituting the single stroke accents for crash and bass drum hits. This gives a nice fluid roll that can be used in a range of different musical situations.

Suggested BPM range: 100-200

29: Single Stroke Workout #1

(Two-bar phrase)

A combination of single stroke rolls in seven, five and three in 4/4.

Unlike the different stroke rolls usually associated with drum rudiments, there are no double strokes here. Each grouping is played hand-to-hand.

Accenting the first note of each group is optional. You should also practise playing the accent as a rim-shot on the snare drum.

It's always good to practise single stroke exercises like this to a quarter note pulse. Play the bass drum on all 4 beats of the bar and work the sticking around it.

As this exercise is played hand-to-hand, it's possible to get the tempo high without too much strain.

Suggested BPM range: 50-110

30: Marching With The Ruffs

(One-bar phrase)

Mix up this exercise by switching the leading hand in each bar.

Take it to the kit and add a bass drum and crash to the 1/8th and 1/4 notes.

When you have the sticking down comfortably, move to the hi-hat to create some interesting beat variations. By adding bass drum and snare you can create a nice syncopated pattern which is musical too.

The main thrust of this pattern will be played on the hi-hat. Move beats 2 and 4 to the snare and add a bass drum on beats 1 and 3, just to establish a basic rhythm.

With this technique, you will be moving from hi-hat to snare following the first 1/16th note triplet. The last note of the bar will also be played on the snare to complete the 4/4 back beat.

You can take a triplet concept like this and use it to spice up regular 1/16th note hi-hat patterns.

Suggested BPM range: 90-180

31: Herbie Returns

(One-bar phrase)

A single stroke workout in fives and threes over two bars.

This symmetrical exercise is notated as 1/32nd notes in 4/4. The first note of each grouping can be accented for more of a challenge.

Play this exercise with and without accents on the first stroke of each grouping. Next move the accent to toms and cymbals.

Use a bass drum pulse to get comfortable playing this warmup in a more syncopated fashion. Single stroke groupings like this are great for incorporating into drum solos.

Be sure to move the sticking around the kit to fully internalise the pattern.

Suggested BPM range: 50-110

32: The Juggler

(One-bar phrase)

Triple strokes in 12/8 combined with three single strokes at the end to complete the bar.

The purpose of this exercise is to get comfortable with the switch from bounce to hand-to-hand sticking.

Use this sticking to sweep between different drums on your setup. One such sweeping motion is to play from snare to floor tom on beat 1. You can play the first 'R' 'L' on the snare and sweep the right-hand to the floor tom to play the next two notes. As you move on to the next beat, reverse this concept, again starting on the snare, but this time moving to the more easily reached front tom.

When you are comfortable with this sweeping motion, try starting on the floor tom and sweeping back to the snare drum.

Suggested BPM range: 70-140

33: Quincey

(One-bar phrase)

Inverted doubles in 5/8.

You don't need to count this warm-up to a metronome at higher tempos, just get the feel of the sticking into your hands from memory and let it flow.

This is another great warm-up that can easily be treated as a one beat phrase. Add a bass drum to the first beat of the bar here and play it close to your maximum speed.

You can substitute this ten-note phrase rhythmically for any standard group of four-, six-, or eight-note rolls. It will take a bit of time to accurately switch between the different note groupings, so to help, think of this phrase musically as opposed to counting each note individually.

Suggested BPM range: 70-180

34: 12/8 Off-beat Pull-outs

(One-bar phrase)

Pull-out accents on the off-beat in 12/8.

This is a trickier example as the accents do not land on the down beats.

For a real challenge, take this sticking to the drum set and aim to make the accents as clear as possible. The different surfaces of the toms should make this even more tricky to pull off.

Another extra-tough exercise is to play every regular note on the hi-hat and every accent on the snare.

Moving in such an unnatural manner like this is great for coordination and builds speed in the upper arms.

Add the bass drum to the first note of each six-note grouping to create a hyper-12/8 kind of feel.

Suggested BPM range: 40-80

35: Snapadiddle Inversion #3

(One-bar phrase)

Last of the Snapadiddle inversions.

The 'snap' lands on the 'a' of each beat. Try not to accent the last beat of each three-note snap. Switch hands and start again.

This pattern works well between a ride, hi-hat snare and bass drum setup. Simply move your leading hand to the ride cymbal and leave your other hand to play the hi-hat.

Add the bass drum on beats 1 and 3. Next, move your leading hand to the snare drum on beat 2 to create a back beat.

You can do the same on beat 4, only this time it will be the opposite hand moving from the hi-hat to play the back beat.

You now have an interesting beat with different rhythms happening in the both right, and left hands.

Suggested BPM range: 110-220

36: Single Stroke Workout #2

(Two-bar phrase)

A nice symmetrical pattern involving sevens and threes.

Keep the four strokes in each leading hand at the same volume.

The key to playing the flurry of notes, particularly the seven-note grouping, is to utilise the bounce from the drum head.

It's easier to use the fingers to create the subsequent strokes at higher tempos.

One modification of this pattern I like to use is to turn each seven-note group into eight by adding one bass drum hit. You can play the entire exercise this way by adding an extra bass drum just after each 1/16th note.

Timing the position of the extra hit can initially be tricky, so take the speed down to around 60 BPM.

Suggested BPM range: 60-110

37: Consecutive Flam 4's

(One-bar phrase)

lR L R rL R L lR L R rL lR rL   rL R L lR L R rL R L lR rL lR

These flams can be played with wrists only or a combination of wrist and finger. Your wrist can play the down-stroke and your fingers can play the grace note… then reverse the sticking.

Use a combination of up-strokes and down-strokes to play flams at higher tempos. Each up-stroke will play the grace note of each flam.

Each down-stroke will play the regular tap.

With time and practice you can train yourself to play flams in this way. There are big advantages to using the up-stroke here: not only does it position your hand properly for the following down-stroke, it also means you can achieve higher speeds and increased fluidity in your playing.

Suggested BPM range: 60-120

38: Inverted Doubles Run

(Two-bar phrase)

Try to keep the inverted roll sounding as smooth as your best single stroke roll. Play with and without the accent on the first stroke of each bar.

One nice application of this warm-up is to keep all accents on the snare only, and the other double strokes on any selection of toms.

Play this between ride and hi-hat for an extra coordination workout. Next place a bass drum on each right-hand stroke.

When you have mastered this exercise, try removing the right hand from the equation to leave just the right foot and left-hand to play an intricate inverted doubles pattern.

Suggested BPM range: 90-180

39: Herta Dublin

(Two-bar phrase)

A combination of 1/16th and 1/8th notes to create a snap/herta symmetrical warm-up.

A clean but relaxed pinch between finger strokes is the key to increasing speed with this exercise.

The first bar of this phrase can be used to play herta-style fills on the drum kit.

One voicing that works well is to play the first two strokes between any two toms. The next two strokes should be played on the snare. Repeat this on the 'and' of beat 2 and finish with three final strokes anywhere you choose.

Splitting the pattern like this is great for mobility around the kit and sounds good too.

Suggested BPM range: 60-130

40: Pulling Teeth

(One-bar phrase)

Consecutive pull-out accents from hand to hand.

Maximize the difference in volume between the quiet and loud notes.

To improve your technique with pull-out accents, move this pattern to the drum set. Play each right-hand accent on the floor tom and each left-hand accent on either front tom or hi-hat. Play every other stroke on the snare drum.

You will need to use a sweeping motion to play the consecutive strokes from snare to tom or snare to hi-hat. The exaggerated motion required to play this sweeping motion will help you build the muscle group that is key to mastering pull-out accents.

Suggested BPM range: 60-120

41: Flamming Moe

(One-bar phrase)

Triple flam exercise.

The flams start on the third 1/16th note and finish on the fifth. Correct stick height is the key to playing each flam:

Grace note – low stick,
Full stroke – high stick.

Play on the snare drum and substitute each flam for cymbal hits. This will mean keeping the grace notes of the flam on the snare drum and the main stroke on ride or hi-hat, depending on your choice.

Using the same concept, substitute the cymbals for other voices such as toms.

Suggested BPM range: 30-110

42: 12/8 Switcheroo

(Two-bar phrase)

R l r r L r l l R l r r L r l l R l r r L r l l R l r L r l R l r L r l l R l r r L r l l R l r r L r l l R l r r L r l R l r L r l

A two-bar phrase written using 1/32nd and 1/16th notes in 12/8.

This example is a modified version of warm-up #17: An extra stroke is added by the opposite hand to embellish each triple stroke.

If you are struggling with the rhythm as notated, return to warm-up #17 and play through it a few times.

The key to mastering the 1/32nd note rhythm is to add one extra note after the first note of each three- and two-note grouping.

Suggested BPM range: 30-80

43: Snappled

(Two-bar phrase)

A 1/32nd note 'Snap' exercise in 4/4.

The rhythm here is designed to be challenging and there are some awkward placements of the snaps. This rhythm becomes easier to grasp at faster tempos.

Counting this exercise in 1/16th notes you can split the bar into groups of 3, 2, 2, 3, 2, 2 and 2.

Accenting the first note of each group allows you to hear the rhythm more clearly.

This warm-up also works well when used in a kit solo. Accent the first note of each group with either toms or cymbals and bass drum combinations.

Suggested BPM range: 60-100

44: Parsnaps

(One-bar phrase)

Switching from snaps to regular doubles.

A useful sticking to play around with on the kit; this warm-up easily translates into some interesting drum fills.

Adding accents to beat 1 and the 'and' of 2 allows you to hear the rhythm of this exercise more easily.

It's also important to practise this idea with reversed sticking.

Play the first hit on the snare followed by tom strokes up until the 'and' of beat 2. Repeating the phrase will take you up to beat 4. Play beat 4 as two snaps on any drums or cymbals you choose.

This sticking works just as well when reversed on the kit too. Start with your left-hand on the snare and play between the floor tom and snare in the same manner as before.

Suggested BPM range: 60-110

45: The Blender

(One-bar phrase)

R L R L R L R L R L L   L R L R L R L R L R R

Combining singles, snaps and doubles.

This pattern works well when moved around the kit and can be played symmetrically for an extra challenge.

You can create an unusual and busy hi-hat groove with this sticking too. Just play the pattern on the hi-hat as normal and place beat 2 on the snare.

When you have the hang of this, you can also add the snare to the 'and' of beat 3. This creates an intricate groove that can also be played around the kit as a drum fill.

Add the bass drum to beats 1, the 'and' of beat 2, and beat 3 for added flavour.

Suggested BPM range: 110-220

46: Trippin' Sevens

(One-bar phrase)

Accents and inverted doubles played over triplets in 7/8.

Play with and without accents. The first two beats here are effectively an inverted six-stroke roll.

This is another warm-up that can easily be taken to the drum kit and expanded upon.

You can also use the sticking to play a kind of halftime shuffle in 7/8. Play the pattern on the hi-hat and move your right-hand to the snare on beats 3 and 7.

Placing a bass drum hit on beats 1 and 5 completes the groove.

You can also build fills around this sticking by playing the accents on toms or crash cymbals with bass drum hits.

Suggested BPM range: 60-110

47: Inverted Seven

(One-bar phrase)

Inverted doubles as 1/32nd notes in 7/8.

The audio example contains accents so the 7/8 pulse is easily heard. Play both with, and without accents.

This pattern is not symmetrical so be sure to switch sticking to start on the opposite hand.

To create a busy 1/32nd note groove, play this pattern between hi-hat and snare. On beat 3, play the first left hand as a clear accent. On beat 7 do the same. These form the basis of the 7/8 groove.

You can add bass drums to any beat for more variation. The easiest are beat 1 and beat 5.

When you have mastered this 1/32nd note groove, try placing additional bass drums on different combinations of other right-hand strokes.

Suggested BPM range: 50-90

48: Inverted Swiss Variation

(One-bar phrase)

Inverted doubles combining with flams to create a one-bar phrase.

Be careful to get the correct sticking on beats 3 and 4.

On the drum set you can work this pattern into a short one-bar groove and fill between ride, snare and toms.

First, play the pattern on the snare drum.

Next, while keeping the exact same sticking, move your right-hand to the ride cymbal. Accent the full stroke of each flam here on the snare (technically the right-hand will be playing the 'grace' note).

The final step is to move each grace note down to the floor tom to complement the snare. You can play this grace note with added volume for a more powerful sound.

Remember to move back to the ride for the subsequent right-hand stroke and repeat the motion. It's only the grace note of the flam that should be played on the floor tom.

Finally, for more definition, add a bass drum to beat 1 and on the 'a' of beat 2.

Suggested BPM range: 60-140

49: Flam Central

(Two-bar phrase)

This warm-up ends with a 'flam tap' on beat 4.

Greater speed can be achieved by using wrist and finger motions in a down/up manner.

Playing this pattern on the drum kit works well with an open snare and warm, full tom sounds. Flams can be played on any voice on the drums, including cymbals.

You might want to use the tip of the drum stick here and play a touch lighter than a standard crash hit.

Suggested BPM range: 50-90

50: Single Stroke Workout #3

(Two-bar phrase)

Singles in groups of seven and three to create a symmetrical warm-up.

Accents can be added to beats 1, 2, 3, the 'and' of 3, and the 'and' of beat 4. Great for endurance runs.

Enhance the accents by playing them with a combination of crash cymbals and bass drums. Play on the snare alone and use rim-shots to voice the accents.

With a bit of practise, you'll find that it's possible to get this pattern up to high tempos. Each grouping has a short pause which allows the hands to recover, unlike an uninterrupted single stroke roll which requires much more stamina.

Use the advantage of switching accents to different hands to create new opportunities for different musical ideas.

Suggested BPM range: 50-110

Conclusion

This book was written with the intention of bringing some inspiration to our practice pads. Most drumming today is still focused around two hands and two sticks. While we know as drummers it can be hard to find a suitable place to play our instrument, it's usually quite easy to find somewhere for your practice pad.

You can play one pattern repeatedly while watching a long movie; mix it up, reverse the sticking, be aware of your weaknesses and work on them... you are training your hands to respond to any musical ideas you can conceive.

One of the pitfalls drummers fall into is becoming too reliant on one side of their playing (either right or left). Each exercise in this book is designed to be mastered on both sides, starting with either hand. By working on this ambidexterity, you free up your musical options on the instrument.

Work on these exercises when you are heading to a gig, practice session, or even if you are feeling a bit uninspired about your playing. When you have spent 5-10 minutes on one warm-up, your hands should be starting to feel more fluid and that's when drumming becomes easier and much more fun.

Further Reading

The following are some recommended books that develop rhythm, technique and drum notation. Some are written for snare drum only and others are designed to accommodate drum kit players.

Rhythm and Notation for Drums – Kev O'Shea

Progressive Steps to Syncopation for the Modern Drummer – Ted Reed

The All-American Drummer – Charley Wilcoxon

The New Breed – Gary Chester

Advanced Funk Studies – Rick Latham

Master Studies – Joe Morello

Advanced Techniques for the Modern Drummer – Jim Chapin

Stick Control – George Lawrence Stone

About the Author

Kev O'Shea has been playing drums and educating drummers worldwide for as long as he can remember and has over 20 years' experience in the music industry.

After studying Jazz in the renowned Newpark Music School of Dublin he has forged a successful career as an in-demand drummer, both live and in the studio.

With many years of extensive touring in Europe, America and the Middle East, Kev brings his expertise to his own website **www.KevOShea.com** where he provides lessons, tips & useful info to his fellow drummers.

Other Books from Fundamental Changes

200 Paradiddle Exercises for Drums

Drum Rudiments and Musical Application

Learn to Play Drums Volume 1

Learn to Play Drums Volume 2

Rhythm Reading and Notation for Drums

Rock Drumming for Beginners

Printed in Great Britain
by Amazon

44249185R00038